Magna Carta

MANUSCRIPTS AND MYTHS

Claire Breay

THE BRITISH LIBRARY

For my parents

First published in 2002
This edition published in 2010 by
The British Library
96 Euston Road
London NW1 2DB

Text © Claire Breay 2010
Illustrations © The British Library Board and other named copyright holders 2010
Translation of Magna Carta on pp.49–54 by G.R.C. Davis

British Library Cataloguing in Publication Data
A catalogue record for this book is available from The British Library

ISBN 978 0 7123 5833 0

Designed and typeset by Andrew Shoolbred
Maps by John Mitchell
Printed in Hong Kong by Great Wall Printing Co. Ltd

Cover illustrations
King John, by Matthew Paris, monk of St Albans, d. 1259
BL Royal MS 14 C. vii, f.9

The 1225 reissue of Magna Carta, granted by Henry III, sent to the county of Wiltshire
and later deposited at Lacock Abbey
BL Add. MS 46144

Image of Runnymede on page 25 ©NTPL/Andrew Butler

Magna Carta

MANUSCRIPTS AND MYTHS

Contents

Chronology

8 January 1198	*Election of Pope Innocent III*
6 April 1199	*Death of King Richard I*
27 May 1199	*Coronation of King John*
March 1204	*Capture of Chateau Gaillard by the French*
March 1208	*Papal Interdict placed on England*
8 November 1209	*King John excommunicated by the pope*
1 June 1213	*King John accepted Stephen Langton as Archbishop of Canterbury*
July 1213	*King John absolved from excommunication*
21 April 1214	*Pope Innocent III accepted the overlordship of England and Ireland*
July 1214	*Defeat of English allies at Bouvines*
January 1215	*Barons petitioned the pope for confirmation of Henry I's charter*
4 March 1215	*King John took the Crusader's oath*
April 1215	*Rebel barons met at Stamford*
17 May 1215	*Rebel barons captured London*
29 May 1215	*King John again rejected the barons' demands*
10 June 1215	*Meeting of King John and the barons at Runnymede began*
15 June 1215	*Magna Carta granted*
19 June 1215	*The barons renewed oaths of allegiance to King John*
24 June 1215	*First seven copies of Magna Carta delivered for distribution*
24 August 1215	*Innocent III issued papal bull declaring Magna Carta null and void*
22 May 1216	*Prince Louis invaded England*
16 July 1216	*Death of Pope Innocent III*
11 October 1216	*Loss of King John's treasure in the Wash*
18/19 October 1216	*Death of King John*
12 November 1216	*William Marshal issued revised version of Magna Carta*
6 November 1217	*Second revision of Magna Carta issued by William Marshal*
11 February 1225	*Third revision of Magna Carta issued under Great Seal of Henry III*
12 October 1297	*Edward I confirmed the 1225 version of Magna Carta: this confirmation was later placed on the first statute roll*

Introduction

No free man shall be seized or imprisoned, or stripped of his rights or possessions, or outlawed or exiled, or deprived of his standing in any other way, nor will we proceed with force against him, or send others to do so, except by the lawful judgement of his equals or by the law of the land.

To no one will we sell, to no one deny or delay right or justice.

These statements, buried deep in the text of King John's Magna Carta, lie at the root of its fame today, but they were not central to its original purpose. Magna Carta – the Great Charter – was not intended to be a lasting declaration of legal principle or theory. It was a practical solution to a political crisis. The dispute between King John and his baronial opponents had reached a stalemate in 1215 and for a few short weeks that summer, Magna Carta seemed to provide a solution.

The charter imposed written constraints on royal authority in the fields of taxation, feudal rights and justice, and it reasserted the power of customary practice to limit unjust or arbitrary behaviour by the king. Over time, its true origin and meaning have become obscured by myths and misunderstandings about its content and significance, as it has come to symbolise principles which played little part in its creation. Despite all the claims which have been made for it since, the charter was not intended to be the cornerstone of English democracy, still less the foundation of a code of human rights. But it was the ways in which the charter was used after the death of King John, rather than the events of 1215, which guaranteed its status and longevity. Although its meaning has been distorted by the interpretations of succeeding generations, it was undoubtedly the intrinsic adaptability of certain key clauses which allowed Magna Carta to be elevated to the iconic status which it has long enjoyed. This book will explore the context in which Magna Carta came to be issued, in order to understand what it really meant to its creators and to those who have used and revered it since.

King John at War

King John was the youngest son of Henry II who, through a combination of inheritance, conquest and marriage, had accumulated extensive territories occupying much of western France from Normandy and Brittany in the north, through Maine, Anjou, Touraine, Poitou and Aquitaine, to Gascony and the Pyrenees in the south. John's elder brother, Richard I, was captured and imprisoned by the German emperor on his return from the Third Crusade to Jerusalem but, after being ransomed in 1194, he successfully defended the majority of Henry II's gains in France in the latter part of his reign.

John succeeded Richard as King of England in April 1199, following Richard's death while besieging the castle of Châlus near Limoges. The King of France, Philip Augustus, was determined to attack the extensive Angevin empire held by the English and he renewed hostilities soon after John's accession. The ensuing series of wars was disastrous for John, despite his strong army of mercenaries. In March 1204, following a short siege, the French captured the supposedly impregnable castle of Gaillard at Les Andelys on the River Seine. This defeat was followed by the surrender

Left: Château Gaillard, Les Andelys, France
Mary Evans Picture Library

Opposite above: King John, as depicted in a catalogue of the benefactors of St Albans Abbey, fifteenth century
BL Cotton Nero D. vii, f. 5v

Opposite below: South view of Westminster Abbey, scene of King John's Coronation, T. Bowles, 1753
BL Map Library, K. Top. XXIV. 4g

JOHN, KING OF ENGLAND

John was the youngest son of Henry II and Eleanor of Aquitaine. Born on Christmas Eve 1167, he succeeded his elder brother, Richard I, as King of England and was crowned at Westminster on 27 May 1199. Events in his reign were dominated by a string of largely unsuccessful and extremely costly continental battles, in which he tried in vain to defend the extensive Angevin empire which he had inherited from his brother. The enormous expense of fighting this continental war encouraged John to exploit his feudal rights and impose extortionate financial demands on the nobility and royal office-holders. His reign was also marked by conflict with the pope, leading to the papal Interdict of 1208–13 which saw the withdrawal of all spiritual services by the clergy. Although an able king with a keen interest in the detail of administration and justice, he could also be capricious and arbitrary. The issuing of Magna Carta in 1215 is the event in his reign for which he is now best remembered.

He married Avice of Gloucester in 1189, but shortly after becoming king he divorced her and married Isabella of Angoulême on 24 August 1200. Their eldest son became King Henry III following John's death at Newark in Nottinghamshire on the night of 18/19 October 1216. John was buried, in accordance with his wishes, in Worcester Cathedral.

THE KINGS OF ENGLAND, 1066–1399

The Normans		The Angevins	
1066–1087	William I, 'the Conqueror'	1154–1189	Henry II
1087–1100	William II, 'Rufus'	1189–1199	Richard I, 'the Lion-heart'
1100–1135	Henry I	1199–1216	John
1135–1154	Stephen	1216–1272	Henry III
		1272–1307	Edward I
		1307–1327	Edward II
		1327–1377	Edward III
		1377–1399	Richard II

France in the time of King John

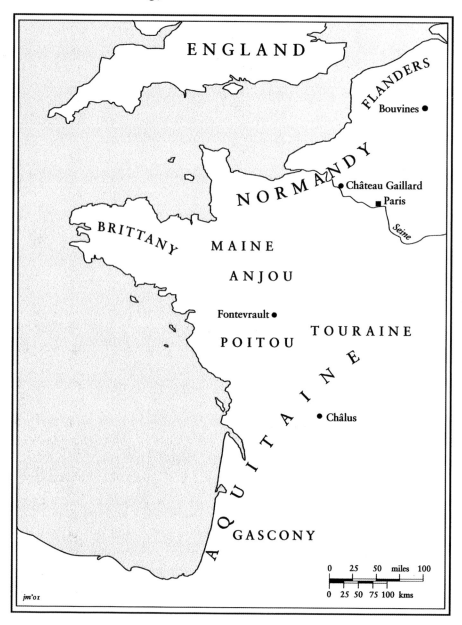

PHILIP II AUGUSTUS, KING OF FRANCE

Philip, the son of Louis VII and Adela of Champagne, succeeded his
father as king in 1180 and went on the Third Crusade with Richard I
of England. Philip is remembered for his firm, centralising government
and for the destruction of the Angevin empire which, at the beginning
of his reign, extended across the western half of France. His success in
wars with King John enabled him to add Normandy, Anjou and part of
Poitou to his domain. By these victories, he added to his earlier acquisition
of Artois, by marriage, and much of Vermandois, by war against the Count of
Flanders. In 1214, Philip successfully defeated a counter-attack by the English allies
at Bouvines. In May 1216 his son, Louis, invaded England but was not able to sustain
the initial support of the barons. Nevertheless, before his death in 1223, Philip had emphatically
confirmed the French monarchy's national leadership and influence.

Above right: Philip
Augustus
BL Harl. 3687, f. 123r

of Falaise, Caen and Rouen, so that by the end of June 1204 the Channel
Islands were the only part of the Duchy of Normandy still held by the
English. The loss of Normandy gravely injured John's prestige: the patri-
mony of William the Conqueror, Duke of Normandy and King of England,
had been broken in two. Quite apart from the severe blow to John's reputa-
tion, the loss of the lands of Normandy also deprived him of the substantial
revenue which they had generated for the Crown, forcing John to extract
even more money from England and Ireland in order to defend England
from invasion and finance his plans for reconquest.

In 1213, the threat of a French invasion of England hung over
John, forcing him to rally an army in Kent, but in the spring the English
naval victory over the French fleet at the Flemish port of Damme gave John
a temporary reprieve. He took the initiative and launched a counter-inva-
sion of France the following year, but in July 1214, ten years after the loss of
Normandy, John suffered an even more catastrophic defeat at Bouvines in
Flanders when Philip Augustus overcame an army of John's allies, including his nephew, Emperor Otto of Brunswick, the Count of Flanders and the
Duke of Brabant. This defeat led to the irrecoverable loss of Anjou, Maine
and Touraine, the heartlands of the Angevin empire, and shattered John's
hopes of ever reconquering his Norman lands. Of the vast territories in
France he had inherited, John retained only Poitou and Gascony by the end
of 1214.

The Feudal King

Warfare has always been an expensive business and the series of battles which John fought to defend his continental inheritance, together with his extensive use of mercenaries, placed an intolerable strain on his Exchequer in a period of rampant inflation. To make matters worse, each time John lost lands in France, he also lost a source of revenue so that the burden of supporting the next military campaign fell on an ever-shrinking number of subjects. In addition to his continental wars, John also pursued campaigns in Ireland, Wales and Scotland. Although more successful, these further military engagements inevitably made his financial crisis even more acute. In an attempt to meet the crippling cost of these wars, John directed his energies to wringing as much revenue as possible from all royal sources of income. He extracted money from administrative office-holders, from the courts and from the feudal system of land tenure.

The sheriffs made an annual payment, known as a farm, to the king. This farm was a compounded payment of all the Crown's ancient rents and dues from its lands in the counties. Sheriffs were prepared to pay huge sums of money to hold the office, because it afforded many opportunities for personal profit, but John antagonised the sheriffs by forcing them to pay ever greater sums on appointment and by adding surcharges to their farms of the counties.

The king also made money from the justice system. Quite apart from the complex system of fines for both infringements of the law and procedural irregularities, litigants sometimes offered large sums in the hope of a favourable decision in the king's courts. In addition to the main system of justice, medieval kings also profited from the laws governing the royal forests. These forests covered vast and relentlessly increasing areas of countryside set aside for hunting by the king and his followers. They were governed by a separate set of especially severe laws, whose punitive fines could be particularly lucrative for the Crown.

The feudal system of land tenure offered even greater opportunities for extortion to an unscrupulous king who was prepared to disregard the constraints of custom. In the feudal hierarchy, all land was ultimately held 'in fee' from the king, in a complex web of tenancies and subtenancies which stretched down from the king's tenants-in-chief, through a series of

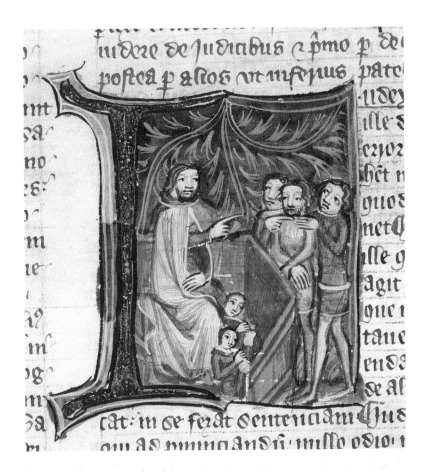

lesser lords, to the rural peasantry – known as the villeins – at the foot of the
pyramid. Everyone in the hierarchy, from the king to the villeins, possessed
rights and owed obligations, both of which were regulated by long-estab-
lished custom. King John fell foul of the barons by repeatedly breaching
custom in his extortionate demands.

The king made money from the return to the Crown of the lands of
tenants who died without heirs and the forfeiture of the lands of convicted
felons. These continual returns, known as escheats, provided him with a
regular supply of land available to grant to others. This source of income
was valuable but could not easily be increased by the king. However, he
was also entitled to 'feudal incidents', a series of the payments due to him
from his tenants-in-chief. Two such incidents were payments called 'aids'
and 'reliefs', and John exploited his right to these payments to the full. The
king could demand an aid in an emergency or on an occasion such as the
marriage of his eldest daughter, whilst heirs and heiresses had to pay a relief

in order to succeed to their estates. For example, King John required Roger de Lacy to pay £4,500 to succeed to his father's lands. This figure was an enormous sum, equal to almost half the king's annual income from the sheriffs' farms of the counties. Nicholas de Stuteville was forced to pay the even greater relief of £6,666 for succession to his lands. In order to meet the demand, Nicholas had to lease some estates, sell others and surrender Knaresborough and Boroughbridge to the king to guarantee payment.

icident was the right of wardship which arose
; an heir who had not yet come of age. Rights of
ble and could be sold by the king to the highest
) exploit the heir's estates for his own short-term
ed estate for the heir to inherit when he came of
also gave the king control over the marriages of
resses. Widows who wished to remarry someone
to pay for the right to do so; some even had to
in unmarried. John's desperate need for income
as much profit as possible from these rights of

ted 'scutage' beyond the bounds of custom.
wed by feudal tenants in lieu of the provision of
. The revenue it generated was used to help meet
paying mercenaries to fight abroad. Whereas
l sought only eight scutages in thirty-four years,
only seventeen years on the throne. As well as
re frequently than had been customary, he also
seen. For example, in anticipation of his attempt
ce in 1214, John levied scutage at the unprece-
dentedly high rate of 3 marks (£2) per knight's fee. The money was due at the end of September but, following the humiliating defeat at Bouvines, many refused to pay.

In his desperation to increase his revenue, John became increasingly unscrupulous in the collection of debts. He enforced his exactions by seizing land, taking hostages and imprisoning defaulters. William de Braose, an important baron in Sussex and the Welsh Marches, failed to keep

Opposite: King John, hunting with dogs
BL Cotton Claudius D. ii, f. 116r

up payments for lands in Ireland and castles in the Marches. In 1209, John forced him to pledge his lands, surrender his castles, and give hostages in an attempt to recover the debts. William tried to resist the king by force: he raised a rebellion in Wales in 1210 and was pursued through Ireland by John but died in France the following year, his wife and son having allegedly been starved to death in Windsor Castle.

The king's willingness to ignore custom and abuse his rights eventually led other baronial victims of his behaviour to rebel against him. He was justifiably nervous of plots by malcontents, and in 1212 there was an unsuccessful conspiracy to assassinate him involving Robert Fitz Walter and Eustace de Vesci, who were prominent in the rebellion of 1215. This plot seems to have had scant effect on his treatment of the barons, and the more unjustly he behaved, the more he encouraged his opponents to organise themselves against him.

King John and the Church

John was King of England more than three centuries before the Reformation, which saw the rejection of papal supremacy by the English Church. His reign from May 1199 to October 1216 coincided almost exactly with the pontificate of Innocent III who was elected pope in January 1198 and died a few months before John in July 1216. For much of his reign, John was engaged in a prolonged dispute with Innocent III, England's spiritual overlord. The means by which John resolved this dispute were unorthodox, to say the least, but worked to his advantage in the months following his agreement with the barons at Runnymede.

The conflict with the papacy originated in the struggle to elect a new Archbishop of Canterbury following the death of Hubert Walter in July 1205. John entered a prolonged conflict with the monks of Christ Church Canterbury, the bishops of the province and the pope to determine who had the right to appoint Walter's successor. Finally, the pope's nominee, Cardinal Stephen Langton, was elected by the monks towards the end of 1206 and was consecrated by the pope on 17 June 1207. However, John refused to admit Langton to England and drove out the monks of Canterbury. In response, the pope placed an Interdict on England in March 1208: mass could not be celebrated, the sacrament of marriage could not be received, and burials in consecrated ground were not allowed. John retaliated by

POPE INNOCENT III

Born in about 1160, Lotario de' Conti di Segni – a nobleman and a scholar – was elected pope in 1198. During his pontificate, he sought to enforce papal power over secular rulers and to drive out heretics from the church. The policies he pursued in Germany, France and England unequivocally demonstrated his power but promoted deep civil unrest. In ecclesiastical government, his determination to impose his judicial authority over the whole Latin church culminated in the major reforms of the Fourth Lateran Council of 1215. By the time of his death in 1216, Innocent had set in place the framework for the mighty edifice of the thirteenth-century papacy.

pres richard regna son sun frere en ky tens Englet
fuit entredpr. vi. aunz e. iii. quarters e. i. moys par

Opposite: Innocent III
BL Cotton MS Faustina B.
vii, f. 69r

Above: King John
receiving a chalice
from a priest
BL Cotton Vitellius A. xiii,
f. 5v

seizing the lands and vast revenues of the church, but in November 1209 the pope excommunicated him, turning him into a spiritual outcast overnight.

By 1212, John was facing the threat of an invasion of England by Philip Augustus of France in alliance with the Welsh. After six years of stubborn resistance to the pope, John, influenced by rumours of an impending conspiracy, had little choice but to make peace with him on terms which amounted to a virtual surrender. As a result, in 1213, he agreed to accept

STEPHEN LANGTON, ARCHBISHOP OF CANTERBURY

Stephen Langton, who was born around 1150, studied and taught at the university in Paris. He was a contemporary of the future Pope Innocent III who made him a cardinal-priest in 1206. The death of Archbishop Hubert Walter in July 1205 left the see of Canterbury vacant but it was not until 17 June 1207 that Langton was consecrated as his successor, following a lengthy disputed election. However, King John's steadfast opposition to the appointment meant that Langton had to remain in exile at Pontigny in France for five years during the Interdict of 1208–13; he was not admitted to his see until 1213 when John finally agreed to accept him as archbishop.

In the events leading up to and surrounding the granting of Magna Carta in June 1215, Langton was an important mediator between the king and his opponents. Later in 1215, Langton travelled to Rome to attend the Fourth Lateran Council. He subsequently held an important ecclesiastical council at Osney Abbey near Oxford in 1222 and remained politically active in the early years of the reign of Henry III until his death in 1228.

Stephen Langton as Archbishop of Canterbury, to reinstate the exiled clergy and to recompense the Church for his plundering of its revenues. Even more dramatically, he resigned his kingdoms of England and Ireland to the papacy, receiving them back in return for an annual payment to Rome of 1000 marks (£666) and the obligation to pay homage to the pope. Langton was at last able to return to England, after six years on the Continent, and in July 1213 he absolved John from excommunication at Winchester.

The following April, in a document known as a papal bull, Innocent III formally accepted John's surrender of his kingdoms. The pope became feudal as well as spiritual overlord of England and Ireland, but allowed John to rule them on his behalf. This desperate act of capitulation by John turned out to have been a very astute decision. Not only was he able to hold on to his throne, but one of his greatest opponents was immediately transformed into his staunchest supporter. Faced with this new alliance, the threat of a French invasion ebbed away. John secured an even greater degree of protection from the Church for himself and his possessions on 4 March 1215 when he took the cross as a crusader. But the usefulness to John of his new relationship to the pope was demonstrated most dramatically in the events which followed the granting of Magna Carta.

Above: Stephen Langton, as depicted on his seal
BL Detached Seal LV. 78

Opposite: Papal bull of Innocent III accepting King John's resignation of England and Ireland
BL Cotton Ch. viii. 24

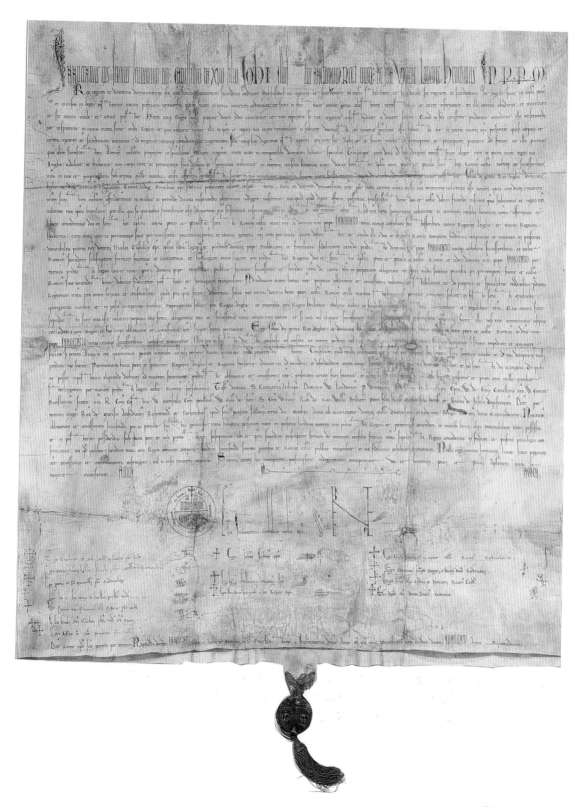

The Road to Runnymede

By Christmas 1214, following the disastrous campaign in France the previous summer, John was faced with demands from the barons for the confirmation of the laws of Edward the Confessor and the charter of liberties which Henry I had issued at his coronation in 1100. The defeat at Bouvines had given the more disaffected barons the opportunity to oppose the increasing centralisation of government under the Angevin kings. By the end of 1214, the rebel barons, who were particularly numerous in northern and eastern England, far outnumbered the minority of loyalists, such as William Marshal, Earl of Pembroke, and Ranulf de Blundeville, Earl of Chester, who supported the king throughout. In January 1215, a group of barons petitioned the pope, in his capacity as England's feudal overlord. Protesting against the excessive scutage of the previous year, they sought confirmation of Henry I's charter and became embroiled in a prolonged struggle with the king for papal support. Meanwhile, Archbishop Stephen Langton encouraged the discontented barons to press John to govern within the bounds of custom, but instead, as John's disputes with his barons intensified, he began hiring continental mercenaries and fortifying castles.

Below: Tomb of William Marshal, the Temple, London
Guildhall Library, Corporation of London

WILLIAM MARSHAL

William Marshal, 4th Earl of Pembroke, was probably born in 1146. He was foremost among King John's loyalists and was one of the chief mediators in the years leading up to 1215. Following John's sudden death in 1216, he was appointed to rule England during the minority of Henry III, who was only nine years old when he came to the throne. He was responsible for securing the two reissues of the revised Magna Carta in 1216 and 1217, but died soon afterwards in 1219.

Places in England associated with Magna Carta

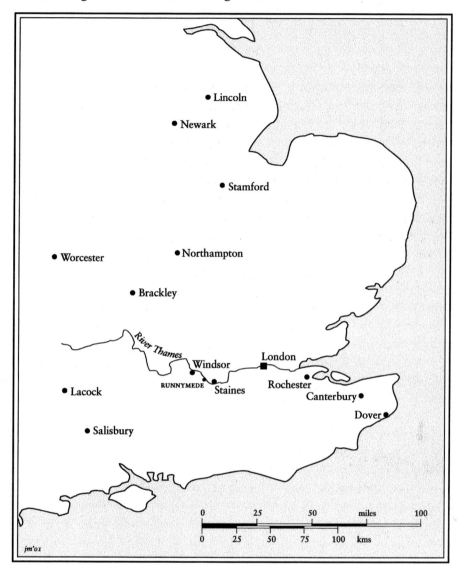

At Easter 1215, some of the barons met at Stamford in Lincolnshire and went on to Northampton for a meeting with John on 26 April. The king failed to arrive. Although he subsequently dismissed some of the soldiers he had been mustering, he continued his refusal to address the barons' demands. On 5 May a group of rebel barons met at Brackley, north of Oxford, and renounced their allegiance to the king. In effect, they had declared civil war. John responded by ordering the seizure of the rebels'

lands and, on 9 May, he proposed that their dispute should be settled by arbitrators chosen by both sides and by the pope, but the barons dismissed this suggestion. The barons tried and failed to take the royal castle at Northampton, but marched on London and captured the Tower on 17 May. This pivotal success greatly strengthened their position and attracted others to their cause, but on 29 May John yet again rejected their demands.

Behind these open exchanges between the king and the barons, it seems that more covert negotiations were also taking place between Archbishop Langton, a proponent of reform, and William Marshal, one of the king's most loyal supporters. As a result of these interventions, by 10 June 1215 a party of barons dressed in full armour had arrived to meet the king's representatives at Runnymede, a meadow by the River Thames between the barons' camp at Staines and the royal castle at Windsor. The detailed negotiations held there led to an agreement involving many concessions by the king which were summarised in an undated document called the Articles of the Barons. The forty-nine articles listed in the document seem to have been the result of detailed preliminary negotiations, not least because the final clause established a commission of twenty-five barons with unprecedented and wide-ranging powers to enforce the king's compliance and constrain his authority. It was long believed, and may indeed be the case, that the barons presented the Articles to the king at Runnymede,

Opposite: The Tower of London, as depicted *c.*1500
BL Royal 16 F. ii, f. 73r

Right: Runnymede

where John sealed them on 15 June. However, it is possible that the Articles predated the meeting by the Thames, and that they were sealed by the king in advance to demonstrate his agreement to their basic demands, in order to bring the opposing parties together for a final settlement. The Articles had no lasting importance, as they were soon superseded by Magna Carta itself, but unlike the original copies of Magna Carta, which were produced by the royal chancery, the Articles must have been handled by the protagonists in the negotiations at Runnymede in June 1215. The document survives to this day: it was lodged by Stephen Langton in the archives of the archdiocese of Canterbury and is now preserved at the British Library in London.

The exact sequence of events at Runnymede remains unclear. The four surviving copies of Magna Carta all bear the date 15 June 1215, which may be the date on which the Articles of the Barons were sealed, or, if that event had already taken place, it may be the date on which further details of the settlement were agreed. Whichever is the case, in the days following 15 June, officials from the royal chancery drafted the full text of Magna Carta from the agreements reached at Runnymede. In common with other medieval charters, Magna Carta bore the date of the agreement itself, not the date of the subsequent issue of the charter by the king. Whatever the precise details of the sequence of events may have been – and these will probably never be certain – on 19 June the barons made formal peace with the king by renewing their oaths of allegiance.

What Was in Magna Carta?

Magna Carta – the Great Charter – was not a statement of fundamental principles of liberty, but a series of concessions addressing long-standing baronial grievances and condemning arbitrary government. Most of its clauses dealt with the limits of the king's rights in specific areas of feudal taxation and administration, but very few were worded as precise statements of the law. It was the product of months of bargaining and its principal beneficiaries were the highest ranks of feudal society. An English translation of the text is printed in full on pages 49–54.

The first of the sixty-three clauses of Magna Carta, granted and confirmed that 'the English Church shall be free, and shall have its rights undiminished, and its liberties unimpaired'. This clause, which did not appear in the Articles of the Barons, confirmed the right of the Church to elect its own bishops and other officials, without royal interference. It reflected the powerful influence of Archbishop Langton who was clearly eager to confirm the rights and freedoms of the Church, which John had challenged so persistently earlier in his reign.

About two-thirds of the remaining clauses in Magna Carta focused on the royal abuses of feudal custom, and provided means for obtaining redress. These clauses did not abolish the king's rights, but moderated and regulated them. For example, the second clause in Magna Carta dealt with the fee payable by an heir for access to his or her inheritance following the death of the previous landholder. Magna Carta fixed this fee, or relief, at £100 for the heir of an earl and a maximum of 100 shillings (£5) for the heir of a knight. The next clause prevented the king from exacting any relief from heirs who were minors when they came of age and inherited their lands. Magna Carta also limited royal powers of wardship over minors and defined the rights of widows in detail. It went on to deal with the particularly contentious issue of scutage, setting out the circumstances in which it could be levied and how the consent of the bishops, abbots, earls and barons for the tax was to be obtained.

In addition to addressing issues of feudal custom and taxation, Magna Carta also dealt with the barons' legal grievances, in particular their exposure to the arbitrary will of the king in matters of justice and his use of judicial disputes to extort huge fines from them. After a clause which stated

THE ADVISERS OF KING JOHN, IN THE ORDER LISTED IN MAGNA CARTA

Stephen Langton, Archbishop of Canterbury

Henry of London, Archbishop of Dublin

William of Sainte-Mère-Église, Bishop of London

Peter des Roches, Bishop of Winchester

Jocelin of Wells, Bishop of Bath and Glastonbury

Hugh of Wells, Bishop of Lincoln

Walter de Gray, Bishop of Worcester

William Cornhill, Bishop of Coventry

Benedict of Sawston, Bishop of Rochester

Pandulf, Subdeacon and member of the pope's household

Aimeric, Master of the Knighthood of the Temple in England

William Marshal, Earl of Pembroke

William Longespée, Earl of Salisbury

William de Warenne, Earl of Surrey

William d'Aubigny, Earl of Arundel

Alan of Galloway, Constable of Scotland

Warin Fitz Gerold

Peter Fitz Herbert

Hubert de Burgh, Seneschal of Poitou

Hugh de Neville

Matthew Fitz Herbert

Thomas Basset

Alan Basset

Philip d'Aubigny

Robert of Ropsley

John Marshal

John Fitz Hugh

that no official was to put a man on trial on the basis of his own unsubstantiated statement, came what are now the two most famous clauses of all. The first prohibited the king from imprisoning, outlawing, exiling or proceeding with force against any free man except by the lawful judgement of his equals or by the law of the land, whilst the second forbade the king from selling, denying or delaying right or justice. Although these are now the most celebrated clauses in Magna Carta, in 1215 they were the thirty-ninth and fortieth clauses in a list of sixty-three: they were not given any special emphasis in the sequence of the king's concessions. For the barons, they were two of the many serious grievances which they were campaigning against, but in succeeding centuries these two clauses were singled out for special treatment as statements of fundamental principles of law.

Magna Carta met most of the grievances of the barons, but it did not fully address the two main concerns of the lesser landholders, who lay immediately below them in the social hierarchy. They wanted action to

Overleaf: Magna Carta, 15 June 1215
BL Cotton MS Augustus ii. 106

restrain the malpractices of sheriffs and other office-holders, who were able to exploit their positions for personal profit, and reductions in the extent of the royal forests which were governed by harsh and punitive laws. Although Magna Carta offered limited concessions in these areas, which were extended in the reissue of 1217 and the Charter of the Forest of the same year, Henry III subsequently reversed or denied many of these gains after he came of age in 1227. This reassertion of the rights of the Crown demonstrated that neither Magna Carta nor the Charter of the Forest were final settlements: both were to prove the subject of ongoing contention in the thirteenth century.

Whilst Magna Carta provided only limited concessions to the lesser landholders and the freemen of England, the peasantry who constituted the mass of the population were firmly outside its remit. However, a minority of clauses dealt with the concerns of special interest groups, rather than those of feudal landholders. Two clauses addressed the issue of debts owed to Jewish money-lenders; another required the removal of fish-weirs throughout England to improve the navigation of rivers; and some dealt with the interests of town-dwellers. These included a clause guaranteeing the

THE TWENTY-FIVE BARONS OF MAGNA CARTA

Richard, Earl of Clare
William de Fors, Count of Aumale
Geoffrey de Mandeville, Earl of Gloucester
Saer de Quincey, Earl of Winchester
Henry de Bohun, Earl of Hereford
Roger Bigod, Earl of Norfolk
Robert de Vere, Earl of Oxford
William Marshall junior
Robert Fitz Walter
Gilbert de Clare
Eustace de Vescy
Hugh Bigod
William de Mowbray

The Mayor of London
William de Lanvallei
Robert de Ros
John de Lacy, Constable of Chester
Richard de Percy
John Fitz Robert
William Malet
Geoffrey de Say
Roger de Montbegon
William of Huntingfield
Richard de Munfichet
William d'Aubigny of Belvoir

ancient liberties and customs of London and all other boroughs, towns and ports; a clause defining the rights of merchants to trade in England; and provision for the standardisation of weights and measures.

In order to guarantee that the text to be issued by the king did not vary from that agreed with the barons, the king provided written security in the form of a copy of the agreement sealed by the Archbishops of Canterbury and Dublin, other bishops and Pandulf, the papal legate. Clause 62 of Magna Carta stated that this document, subsequently known as the 'letters testimonial', was sealed before the copies of Magna Carta were sent out. Unfortunately, the original letters testimonial seem to have been lost. An inventory records that they were lodged in the Exchequer in the fourteenth century, but the text is now known only through a transcription included in the collection of documents copied into the Red Book of the Exchequer.

Perhaps the most radical clause in Magna Carta was that which provided for the election of a commission of twenty-five barons to monitor the king's compliance with the settlement and to enforce its terms. To ensure that enforcement was possible, the twenty-five barons were empowered to seize the king's lands and possessions if he failed to adhere to the conditions imposed on him. The commission lost no time in settling a large number of outstanding legal disputes affecting the barons and, although it did not appear in the reissues of Magna Carta, the justices continued to decide such cases without reference to the king both before and after Henry III reached his majority in 1227. The creation of the commission and the terms under which it operated confirmed the whole tenor of Magna Carta: the law was a power in its own right and the king could not set himself above it.

The Documents

One of the most frequently asked questions concerning the four surviving copies of Magna Carta is, 'Which one is the original?' In fact, there is no evidence at all to suggest that a single, original Magna Carta was ceremonially sealed at Runnymede in June 1215, nor even that such a document ever existed. Rather, it seems that scribes in the royal chancery expanded and revised the draft settlement agreed at Runnymede by 19 June, and turned it into a charter with sixty-three clauses. In common with other medieval charters, Magna Carta took the form of a legal letter, recording agreements which the parties had already made verbally. Each copy of Magna Carta produced in the royal chancery was a record which confirmed and provided retrospective evidence of the settlement made at Runnymede.

The first seven copies of the sealed grant produced by the royal chancery were delivered for distribution on 24 June. It is likely that, as with other royal grants, the acquisition of a copy of Magna Carta was dependent

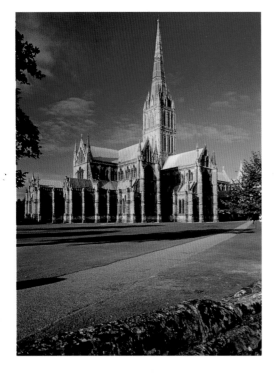

on the payment of fees by the recipient. According to contemporary chroniclers, the recipients included both sheriffs of the counties and bishops. A chancery writ of 19 June informed the sheriffs that peace had been made and that the resulting charter was to be read out in public. The issue of thirteen copies is recorded but exactly how many more copies were sent out from the royal chancery in 1215 is obscure. Only four are now known to survive. Two of the four are held in the British Library, one is preserved in the archives of Lincoln Cathedral and another in the archives of Salisbury Cathedral. The copy of Magna Carta held in Lincoln has remained in the county to which it was originally sent in 1215 as, in all probability, has the copy in Salisbury. The recipients – either the bishop or the sheriff – doubtless lodged their copy in the local cathedral archives for safekeeping. The two copies held in the British Library came from the collection of the notable antiquary, Sir Robert Cotton (1571–1631). One of these copies was given to

Opposite left:
Salisbury Cathedral
Salisbury Cathedral/
Steve Day

Opposite right:
Lincoln Cathedral
Edward Way

Right: The British
Library, London
The British Library

Cotton by Humphrey Wyems, or Wymes, of the Inner Temple in London on 1 January 1629; according to one account, this copy had been discovered in a London tailor's shop. The other British Library copy was found amongst the records of Dover Castle and sent to Cotton by Sir Edward Dering in 1630. This copy is presumably the one which is recorded as having been sent to the Barons of the Cinque Ports on or after 24 June 1215. Unfortunately, it is now virtually illegible, having been badly damaged in 1731 in a fire at Ashburnham House, Westminster, where the Cotton Library was then housed.

All four surviving copies of Magna Carta are of different size and shape, and each has slight variations in the text. Nonetheless, all four documents have equal weight: none can claim greater textual authority than the other three. The Salisbury Magna Carta does differ from the others in that it was not written in the hand of a scribe of the royal chancery. This may mean that it was produced by its recipient and presented for authorisation under the Great Seal, but its text is as authentic as the other three.

Magna Carta, in common with other medieval charters, was written on sheets of parchment. The parchment was manufactured from sheepskin which was soaked in a bath of lime, stretched on a frame to dry under tension, and scraped with a crescent-shaped knife called a lunular to produce a smooth writing surface. The scribes wrote on the parchment using a quill pen made from a long feather and ink produced by mixing iron salts with a caustic liquid extracted from galls on oak trees. The text of

A medieval scribe in an early fifteenth-century manuscript
BL Royal MS 17 E. iii, f. 145r

The production
of parchment,
illustrated
in a thirteenth-
century German
manuscript

Copenhagen, Kongelige
Bibliotek, MS 4, 2°,
f. 183v

Magna Carta was written in heavily-abbreviated Latin, in the handwriting
of the early thirteenth century.

King John did not sign the copies of Magna Carta which were
issued from the royal chancery in 1215. In fact, although we know that
John could read, and indeed borrowed books from monastic libraries, there
is no evidence at all that he could write. Like other medieval charters, the
copies of Magna Carta were authenticated not with a signature, but by the
application of a seal, in this case the king's Great Seal. The Great Seal was
also affixed to the Articles of the Barons, which were the subject of negotia-
tion at Runnymede.

The sealing of royal charters was the task of a chancery official
known as the spigurnel. The seal was made from beeswax and resin and
was attached to the charter with plaited cords. Most medieval seals were
single-sided and were made by pressing a softened quantity of wax into the
seal matrix or die which bore the design of the seal. However, the royal
Great Seal was a large, double-sided seal. Impressions were made with two

Above: Medieval
seal press
Canterbury Cathedral
Library

Below: Impression
of King John's
Great Seal
By permission of the
Provost and Fellows of
Eton College

equal-sized matrices, one for each side of the seal, which were clamped together using a large seal press, such as the one preserved at Canterbury Cathedral. Two circles of wax were prepared and one was placed into each half of the matrix. The two halves were aligned, one above the other, using the rings and pins around their edges. The cords for attaching the seal to the document were laid between the two halves which were then placed into the seal press. The press was tightened, forming the impressions on both sides of the seal and joining the two halves together.

King John's Great Seal measured 95 millimetres (about four inches) in diameter: it added weight, both literally and symbolically, to Magna Carta. The front of the seal, known as the obverse, illustrates the majestic power of the king, showing him crowned and seated on a throne, holding a sword in his right hand and an orb in his left. The reverse of the seal shows the king on horseback, prepared for combat, wearing a coat of mail and helmet, brandishing a sword in his right hand and a spear in his left. Of the four remaining copies of Magna Carta, only one still retains its seal. Unfortunately, this is the copy damaged in the Cotton Library fire of 1731 whose heat reduced the seal to a shapeless lump of wax. The seal on the Articles of the Barons has fared better: although no longer attached to the document, it has survived intact.

Magna Carta after June 1215

By granting Magna Carta, John had allowed the power of the king to be limited by a written document. This had never happened before, but John was just playing for time. Although he had promised not to attempt to have Magna Carta revoked by any third party, he was confident that the pope – England's new feudal overlord – would never agree to such restrictions on his authority. In July he sent envoys to Innocent III seeking an annulment of the charter and, before most of its terms could be properly implemented, the pope issued a document, known as a papal bull, declaring it null and void. The bull, dated 24 August 1215, arrived in England around the end of September. It stated that Magna Carta was 'as unlawful and unjust as it is base and shameful ... whereby the Apostolic See is brought into contempt, the royal prerogative diminished, the English outraged, and the whole enterprise of the Crusade gravely imperilled'. Magna Carta had been legally valid for only ten weeks.

Within months of the pope's denunciation, England was embroiled in an even worse civil war than the one which Magna Carta had sought to avert. John demanded that Archbishop Langton should surrender the royal castle at Rochester which was in his keeping. Langton refused and in September the governor of the castle handed it over to the rebel barons. John besieged the castle for seven weeks until he eventually captured it on

Below: North-west view of Rochester Castle, Kent, by S. and N. Buck, 1735
BL Map Library, K. Top. XVII. 10m

Opposite: A castle under siege in the early fourteenth century
BL Royal MS 16 G. vi, f. 345v

30 November, but in the following months he faced further rebellions, particularly in the eastern and northern counties.

Although a minority of the barons – including the earls of Pembroke and Chester – remained loyal to John, towards the end of 1215 a group of rebellious barons offered the English throne to Louis, son of Philip Augustus, in return for French support. Philip was not inclined to break his truce with John by supporting a French invasion and was wary of antagonising the pope, but Louis sent over a party of knights who joined the rebel stronghold in London. Rather than attempting to recapture the city of London, John decided to undertake an expedition throughout the rebels' territory in northern and eastern England. Between December 1215 and March 1216 he successfully suppressed much of his opposition, but still had not tackled the core of the rebellion in London. On 22 May, Prince Louis

A royal feast in an early fourteenth-century French manuscript
BL Add. MS 28162, f. 10v

Tomb of King John
in the choir of
Worcester Cathedral
Photo © Woodmansterne

invaded England and by the summer two thirds of the barons had gone over to the French side, paid homage to Louis and recognised him as king. Despite these rapid initial gains, the French failed in their attempt to capture Dover. Soon afterwards, disputes flared up between the invaders and the native rebels and eventually the English support for the French collapsed.

Encouraged by these events, John decided to go on the offensive in the eastern counties. Following success at Lincoln, he was welcomed at Lynn, but he contracted dysentery there, reportedly as a result of over-indulgence on peaches and new cider. On 11 October 1216, John travelled to Wisbech, and the next day set off for Swineshead in Lincolnshire, but on the way some of his baggage carts loaded with his treasure were lost in the perilous quicksands of the Wash. Only a week later, on the night of 18/19 October 1216, John died suddenly in Newark, having failed to recover from his attack of dysentery. Unlike his father and brothers, who were buried at Fontevrault in France, he asked to be buried in England, at Worcester Cathedral, where his tomb may still be visited.

October 1216 could easily have been the end of Magna Carta since it had been overturned by the pope, the king was dead and John's son and heir, Henry III, was only nine years old. Because Henry was too young to rule independently, William Marshal, Earl of Pembroke, was appointed to govern the country during his minority. To help restore peace to the kingdom, Marshal, who had remained steadfastly loyal to John throughout his reign, lost no time in issuing a revised version of Magna Carta on 12 November 1216, and another with further revisions on 6 November 1217. In this second reissue, the clauses relating to the royal forests were taken out, amplified considerably and issued in a separate Charter of the Forest. It was after this that the charter of liberties became known as Magna Carta – the Great Charter – to distinguish it from the shorter Charter of the Forest.

The reissues of 1216 and 1217 retained much of the original charter, including the clauses relating to feudal incidents and the operation of the judicial system, but they dropped or modified many others, such as the retrospective clauses imposed on John and the provision for a commission of twenty-five barons to enforce adherence to the settlement. By moderating the terms of the charter in this way, William Marshal was able to attract the support of rebel and loyalist barons alike, since almost all the barons were ready to back the programme of reforms as drafted in 1216–17.

In 1225, Henry III made the most significant reissue of the charter. It was the first made under Henry's own Great Seal, rather than under the seals of his advisers, and it had added weight because it was made in return for a grant of taxation to the king. Henry III and his successors repeatedly confirmed the 1225 version of the charter, sometimes adding or altering clauses. In this way, Magna Carta was transformed from a document wrung from a king facing civil war, into the standard royal declaration of the law and custom of the country. In 1297 the text of the 1225 reissue was copied on to the first statute roll. This meant that, despite the revisions made in the decade following 1215, the core of the barons' programme agreed at Runnymede had been officially incorporated into English law.

The issues addressed by Magna Carta retained their importance and in 1253 a document was issued at Westminster Hall declaring that

Magna Carta in a
fourteenth-century
statute book

BL Lansdowne MS
478, ff. 3v-4r

anyone who broke its terms was to be excommunicated. Orders were made for it to be read twice a year in county courts from 1265, and twice yearly in cathedrals from 1297. It was routinely read and confirmed at the opening of each parliament, and in 1341 parliament required the officers of state to swear to observe its terms. The mid-fourteenth century also saw six acts of parliament reinterpreting the famous clause relating to justice, so that 'the lawful judgement of peers' was redefined as trial by peers and therefore trial by jury. The kings of the later Middle Ages continued to issue confirmations of Magna Carta, but it was during the seventeenth century that its significance underwent a profound shift when lawyers argued that it stated fundamental principles of law.

The Stuart kings James I and Charles I believed that they ruled by the Divine Right of Kings and that therefore they did not have to take account of the provisions of Magna Carta. In opposition, lawyers such as Edward Coke, the Lord Chief Justice, insisted that Magna Carta made the king subject to the law like everyone else. But Coke was very selective, choosing to interpret it as a declaration of individual liberty, rather than a code of custom and law serving the interests of the early thirteenth-century barons. He also tried to argue that Magna Carta was the origin of the principle of trial by jury, whereas in fact this process was at only a rudimentary stage of development in 1215. Such arguments reflect Magna Carta's iconic status as a document: they show the extent to which myths surrounding its content and original purpose have grown up over time.

Magna Carta has become such a famous document because it has been interpreted as the first to guarantee basic civil liberties and freedom for all under the law. Some people have even tried to argue that the origin of parliament lay in Magna Carta, whilst in the eighteenth century English radicals cited it in their attacks on oppressive parliaments and tyrannical lawyers. In America, William Penn, founder of the state of Pennsylvania, wrote a commentary on Magna Carta and used parts of it as the basis for the laws of Pennsylvania, whilst the 'injuries and usurpations' listed in the American Declaration of Independence in 1776 included notable resonances of Magna Carta. From the New World, ideas of individual liberty, based on the myth, spread back to Europe and influenced the revolt against the monarchy in the French Revolution.

On 10 December 1948 the United Nations adopted the Universal Declaration of Human Rights, the product of three years of drafting. Several articles in the Declaration are distant echoes of Magna Carta. These include:

Article 3: *Everyone has the right to life, liberty and security of person.*
Article 9: *No one shall be subjected to arbitrary arrest, detention or exile.*
Article 10: *Everyone is entitled in full equality to a fair and public hearing … in the determination of his rights and obligations and of any criminal charge against him.*
Article 17: *No one shall be arbitrarily deprived of his property.*

Edward Coke
Lord Chief Justice
B.1551
D.1633

However, it would be anachronistic in the extreme to argue that the creators of Magna Carta had any thoughts of establishing embryonic human rights. Magna Carta was a response to a political crisis which had been brewing for years and nearly all the grievances which it addressed were those of the highest-ranking feudal landowners in the kingdom, not those of the majority of the population.

Almost the whole of the 1225 version of Magna Carta, which was copied on to the first statute roll in 1297, has since been repealed, as the aspects of medieval land tenure, taxation and administration which it sought to regulate have become obsolete. Only three clauses remain law. These are the first clause, which guarantees that the English church shall be free, with undiminished rights and liberties, and the clause confirming, but not defining, the privileges of the city of London and all other cities, boroughs, towns and ports. But the most important clause which remains unrepealed is the most famous of all: it provides the safeguard of the judgement of one's equals and the law of the land as protection for free men from arbitrary imprisonment, the seizure of their property or the use of force against them, and it prohibits the sale, denial or delaying of justice. It is because of this clause that Magna Carta is still invoked today by politicians, and is still sometimes cited in judgements in courts of law.

Although the events surrounding the creation of Magna Carta were well documented by medieval chroniclers, the myths which have enveloped it in succeeding centuries have undoubtedly tended to obscure its original causes and purpose. But, despite the endless reinterpretations of key clauses, Magna Carta's most enduring legacy is that it established the principle that the king – the highest authority in the land – was subject to the law, and that the limits of the king's authority could be defined by a written document.

The Text of Magna Carta

JOHN, by the grace of God King of England, Lord of Ireland, Duke of Normandy and Aquitaine, and Count of Anjou, to his archbishops, bishops, abbots, earls, barons, justices, foresters, sheriffs, stewards, servants and to all his officials and loyal subjects, Greeting.

KNOW THAT BEFORE GOD, for the health of our soul and those of our ancestors and heirs, to the honour of God, the exaltation of the holy Church and the better ordering of our kingdom, at the advice of our reverend fathers Stephen, archbishop of Canterbury, primate of all England, and cardinal of the holy Roman Church, Henry archbishop of Dublin, William bishop of London, Peter bishop of Winchester, Jocelin bishop of Bath and Glastonbury, Hugh bishop of Lincoln, Walter bishop of Worcester, William bishop of Coventry, Benedict bishop of Rochester, Master Pandulf subdeacon and member of the papal household, Brother Aymeric master of the knighthood of the Temple in England, William Marshal earl of Pembroke, William earl of Salisbury, William earl of Warren, William earl of Arundel, Alan de Galloway constable of Scotland, Warin Fitz Gerald, Peter Fitz Herbert, Hubert de Burgh seneschal of Poitou, Hugh de Neville, Matthew Fitz Herbert, Thomas Basset, Alan Basset, Philip Daubeny, Robert de Roppeley, John Marshal, John Fitz Hugh, and other loyal subjects:

1 ✳ FIRST THAT WE HAVE GRANTED TO GOD, and by this present charter have confirmed for us and our heirs in perpetuity, that the English Church shall be free, and shall have its rights undiminished, and its liberties unimpaired. That we wish this so to be observed, appears from the fact that of our own free will, before the outbreak of the present dispute between us and our barons, we granted and confirmed by charter the freedom of the Church's elections – a right reckoned to be of the greatest necessity and importance to it – and caused this to be confirmed by Pope Innocent III. This freedom we shall observe ourselves, and desire to be observed in good faith by our heirs in perpetuity.

TO ALL FREE MEN OF OUR KINGDOM we have also granted, for us and our heirs for ever, all the liberties written out below, to have and to keep for them and their heirs, of us and our heirs:

2 If any earl, baron, or other person that holds lands directly of the Crown, for military service, shall die, and at his death his heir shall be of full age and owe a 'relief', the heir shall have his inheritance on payment of the ancient scale of 'relief'. That is to say, the heir or heirs of an earl shall pay £100 for the entire earl's barony, the heir or heirs of a knight 100s. at most for the entire knight's 'fee', and any man that owes less shall pay less, in accordance with the ancient usage of 'fees'.

3 But if the heir of such a person is under age and a ward, when he comes of age he shall have his inheritance without 'relief' or fine.

4 The guardian of the land of an heir who is under age shall take from it only reasonable revenues, customary dues, and feudal services. He shall do this without destruction or damage to men or property. If we have given the guardianship of the land to a sheriff, or to any person answerable to us for the revenues, and he commits destruction or damage, we will exact compensation from him, and the land shall be entrusted to two worthy and prudent men of the same 'fee', who shall be answerable to us for the revenues, or to the person to whom we have assigned them. If we have given or sold to anyone the guardianship of such land, and he causes destruction or damage, he shall lose the guardianship of it, and it shall be handed over to two worthy and prudent men of the same 'fee', who shall be similarly answerable to us.

5 For so long as a guardian has guardianship of such land, he shall maintain the houses, parks, fish preserves, ponds, mills, and everything else

pertaining to it, from the revenues of the land itself. When the heir comes of age, he shall restore the whole land to him, stocked with plough teams and such implements of husbandry as the season demands and the revenues from the land can reasonably bear.

6 Heirs may be given in marriage, but not to someone of lower social standing. Before a marriage takes place, it shall be made known to the heir's next-of-kin.

7 At her husband's death, a widow may have her marriage portion and inheritance at once and without trouble. She shall pay nothing for her dower, marriage portion, or any inheritance that she and her husband held jointly on the day of his death. She may remain in her husband's house for forty days after his death, and within this period her dower shall be assigned to her.

8 No widow shall be compelled to marry, so long as she wishes to remain without a husband. But she must give security that she will not marry without royal consent, if she holds her lands of the Crown, or without the consent of whatever other lord she may hold them of.

9 Neither we nor our officials will seize any land or rent in payment of a debt, so long as the debtor has movable goods sufficient to discharge the debt. A debtor's sureties shall not be distrained upon so long as the debtor himself can discharge his debt. If, for lack of means, the debtor is unable to discharge his debt, his sureties shall be answerable for it. If they so desire, they may have the debtor's lands and rents until they have received satisfaction for the debt that they paid for him, unless the debtor can show that he has settled his obligations to them.

10 * If anyone who has borrowed a sum of money from Jews dies before the debt has been repaid, his heir shall pay no interest on the debt for so long as he remains under age, irrespective of whom he holds his lands. If such a debt falls into the hands of the Crown, it will take nothing except the principal sum specified in the bond.

11 * If a man dies owing money to Jews, his wife may have her dower and pay nothing towards the debt from it. If he leaves children that are under age, their needs may also be provided for on a scale appropriate to the size of his holding of lands. The debt is to be paid out of the residue, reserving the service due to his feudal lords. Debts owed to persons other than Jews are to be dealt with similarly.

12 * No 'scutage' or 'aid' may be levied in our kingdom without its general consent, unless it is for the ransom of our person, to make our eldest son a knight, and (once) to marry our eldest daughter. For these purposes only a reasonable 'aid' may be levied. 'Aids' from the city of London are to be treated similarly.

13 * The city of London shall enjoy all its ancient liberties and free customs, both by land and by water. We also will and grant that all other cities, boroughs, towns, and ports shall enjoy all their liberties and free customs.

14 * To obtain the general consent of the realm for the assessment of an 'aid' – except in the three cases specified above – or a 'scutage', we will cause the archbishops, bishops, abbots, earls, and greater barons to be summoned individually by letter. To those who hold lands directly of us we will cause a general summons to be issued, through the sheriffs and other officials, to come together on a fixed day (of which at least forty days notice shall be given) and at a fixed place. In all letters of summons, the cause of the summons will be stated. When a summons has been issued, the business appointed for the day shall go forward in accordance with the resolution of those present, even if not all those who were summoned have appeared.

15 * In future we will allow no one to levy an 'aid' from his free men, except to ransom his person, to make his eldest son a knight, and (once) to marry his eldest daughter. For these purposes only a reasonable 'aid' may be levied.

16 No man shall be forced to perform more service for a knight's 'fee', or other free holding of land, than is due from it.

17 Ordinary lawsuits shall not follow the royal court around, but shall be held in a fixed place.

18 Inquests of *novel disseisin*, *mort d'ancestor*, and *darrein presentment* shall be taken only in their proper county court. We ourselves, or in our absence abroad our chief justice, will send two justices to each county four times a year, and these justices, with four knights of the county elected by the county itself, shall hold the assizes in the county court, on the day and in the place where the court meets.

19 If any assizes cannot be taken on the day of the county court, as many knights and freeholders shall afterwards remain behind, of those who have attended the court, as will suffice for the administration of justice, having regard to the volume of business to be done.

20 For a trivial offence, a free man shall be fined only in proportion to the degree of his offence, and for a serious offence correspondingly, but not so heavily as to deprive him of his livelihood. In the same way, a merchant shall be spared his merchandise, and a husbandman the implements of his husbandry, if they fall upon the mercy of a royal court. None of these fines shall be imposed except by the assessment on oath of reputable men of the neighbourhood.

21 Earls and barons shall be fined only by their equals, and in proportion to the gravity of their offence.

22 A fine imposed upon the lay property of a clerk in holy orders shall be assessed upon the same principles, without reference to the value of his ecclesiastical benefice.

23 No town or person shall be forced to build bridges over rivers except those with an ancient obligation to do so.

24 No sheriff, constable, coroners or other royal officials are to hold lawsuits that should be held by the royal justices.

25 ✳ Every country, hundred, wapentake, and tithing shall remain at its ancient rent, without increase, except the royal demesne manors.

26 If at the death of a man who holds a lay 'fee' of the Crown, a sheriff or royal official produces royal letters patent of summons for a debt due to the Crown, it shall be lawful for them to seize and list movable goods found in the lay 'fee' of the dead man to the value of the debt, as assessed by worthy men. Nothing shall be removed until the whole debt is paid, when the residue shall be given over to the executors to carry out the dead man's will. If no debt is due to the Crown, all the movable goods shall be regarded as the property of the dead man, except the reasonable shares of his wife and children.

27 ✳ If a free man dies intestate, his movable goods are to be distributed by his next-of-kin and friends, under the supervision of the Church. The rights of debtors are to be preserved.

28 No constable or other royal official shall take corn or other movable goods from any man without immediate payment, unless the seller voluntarily offers postponement of this.

29 No constable may compel a knight to pay money for castle-guard if the knight is willing to undertake the guard in person, or with reasonable excuse to supply some other fit man to do it. A knight taken or sent on military service shall be excused from castle-guard for the period of this service.

30 No sheriff, royal official, or other person shall take horses or carts for transport from any free man, without his consent.

31 Neither we nor any royal official will take wood for our castle, or for any other purpose, without the consent of the owner.

32 We will not keep the lands of people convicted of felony in our hand for longer than a year and a day, after which they shall be returned to the lords of the 'fees' concerned.

33 All fish-weirs shall be removed from the Thames, the Medway, and throughout the whole of England, except on the sea coast.

34 The writ called *precipe* shall not in future be issued to anyone in respect of any holding of land, if a free man could thereby be deprived of the right of trial in his own lord's court.

35 There shall be standard measures of wine, ale, and corn (the London quarter), throughout the kingdom. There shall also be a standard width of dyed cloth, russett, and haberject, namely two ells within the selvedges. Weights are to be standardised similarly.

36 In future nothing shall be paid or accepted for the issue of a writ of inquisition of life or limbs. It shall be given *gratis*, and not refused.

37 If a man holds land of the Crown by 'fee-farm', 'socage', or 'burgage', and also holds land of some-one else for knight's service, we will not have guardianship of his heir, nor of the land that belongs to the other person's 'fee', by virtue of the 'fee-farm', 'socage', or 'burgage', unless the 'fee-farm' owes knight's service. We will not have the guardianship of a man's heir, or of land that he holds of someone else, by reason of any small property that he may hold of the Crown for a service of knives, arrows, or the like.

38 In future no official shall place a man on trial upon his own unsupported statement, without producing credible witnesses to the truth of it.

39 * No free man shall be seized or imprisoned, or stripped of his rights or possessions, or outlawed or exiled, or deprived of his standing in any other way, nor will we proceed with force against him, or send others to do so, except by the lawful judgement of his equals or by the law of the land.

40 * To no one will we sell, to no one deny or delay right or justice.

41 All merchants may enter or leave England unharmed and without fear, and may stay or travel within it, by land or water, for purposes of trade, free from all illegal exactions, in accordance with ancient and lawful customs. This, however, does not apply in time of war to merchants from a country that is at war with us. Any such merchants found in our country at the outbreak of war shall be detained without injury to their persons or property, until we or our chief justice have discovered how our own merchants are being treated in the country at war with us. If our own merchants are safe they shall be safe too.

42 * In future it shall be lawful for any man to leave and return to our kingdom unharmed and without fear, by land or water, preserving his allegiance to us, except in time of war, for some short period, for the common benefit of the realm. People that have been imprisoned or outlawed in accordance with the law of the land, people from a country that is at war with us, and merchants – who shall be dealt with as stated above – are excepted from this provision.

43 If a man holds lands of any 'escheat' such as the 'honour' of Wallingford, Nottingham, Boulogne, Lancaster, or of other 'escheats' in our hand that are baronies, at his death his heir shall give us only the 'relief' and service that he would have made to the baron, had the barony been in the baron's hand. We will hold the 'escheat' in the same manner as the baron held it.

44 People who live outside the forest need not in future appear before the royal justices of the forest in answer to general summonses, unless they are actually involved in proceedings or are sureties for some-one who has been seized for a forest offence.

45 * We will appoint as justices, constables, sheriffs, or other officials, only men that know the law of the realm and are minded to keep it well.

46 All barons who have founded abbeys, and have charters of English kings or ancient tenure as evidence of this, may have guardianship of them when there is no abbot, as is their due.

47 All forests that have been created in our reign shall at once be disafforested. River-banks that have been enclosed in our reign shall be treated similarly.

48 * All evil customs relating to forests and warrens, foresters, warreners, sheriffs and their servants, or river-banks and their wardens, are at once to be investigated in every county by twelve sworn knights of the county, and within forty days of their enquiry the evil customs are to be abolished completely and irrevocably. But we, or our chief justice if we are not in England, are first to be informed.

49 * We will at once return all hostages and charters delivered up to us by Englishmen as security for peace or for loyal service.

50 * We will remove completely from their offices the kinsmen of Gerard de Athée, and in future they shall hold no offices in England. The people in ques-tion are Engelard de Cigogné, Peter, Guy, and Andrew

de Chanceaux, Guy de Cicogné, Geoffrey de Martigny and his brothers, Philip Marc and his brothers, with Geoffrey his nephew, and all their followers.

51 * As soon as peace is restored, we will remove from the kingdom all the foreign knights, bowmen, their attendants, and the mercenaries that have come to it, to its harm, with horses and arms.

52 * To any man whom we have deprived or dispossessed of lands, castles, liberties, or rights, without the lawful judgement of his equals, we will at once restore these. In cases of dispute the matter shall be resolved by the judgement of the twenty-five barons referred to below in the clause for securing the peace (§ 61). In cases, however, where a man was deprived or dispossessed of something without the lawful judgement of his equals by our father King Henry or our brother King Richard, and it remains in our hands or is held by others under our warranty, we shall have respite for the period commonly allowed to Crusaders, unless a lawsuit had been begun, or an enquiry had been made at our order, before we took the Cross as a Crusader. On our return from the Crusade, or if we abandon it, we will at once render justice in full.

53 * We shall have similar respite in rendering justice in connexion with forests that are to be disafforested, or to remain forests, when these were first afforested by our father Henry or our brother Richard; with the guardianship of lands in another person's 'fee', when we have hitherto had this by virtue of a 'fee' held of us for knight's service by a third party; and with abbeys founded in another person's 'fee', in which the lord of the 'fee' claims to own a right. On our return from the Crusade, or if we abandon it, we will at once do full justice to complaints about these matters.

54 No one shall be arrested or imprisoned on the appeal of a woman for the death of any person except her husband.

55 * All fines that have been given to us unjustly and against the law of the land, and all fines that we have exacted unjustly, shall be entirely remitted or the matter decided by a majority judgement of the twenty-five barons referred to below in the clause for securing the peace (§61) together with Stephen, archbishop of Canterbury, if he can be present, and such others as he wishes to bring with him. If the archbishop cannot be present, proceedings shall

continue without him, provided that if any of the twenty-five barons has been involved in a similar suit himself, his judgement shall be set aside, and someone else chosen and sworn in his place, as a substitute for the single occasion, by the rest of the twenty-five.

56 If we have deprived or dispossessed any Welshmen of land, liberties or anything else in England or in Wales, without the lawful judgement of their equals, these are at once to be returned to them. A dispute on this point shall be determined in the Marches by the judgement of equals. English law shall apply to holdings of land in England, Welsh law to those in Wales, and the law of the Marches to those in the Marches. The Welsh shall treat us and ours in the same way.

57 * In cases where a Welshman was deprived or dispossessed of anything, without the lawful judgement of his equals, by our father King Henry or our brother King Richard, and it remains in our hands or is held by others under our warranty, we shall have respite for the period commonly allowed to Crusaders, unless a lawsuit had been begun, or an enquiry had been made at our order, before we took the Cross as a Crusader. But on our return from the Crusade, or if we abandon it, we will at once do full justice according to the laws of Wales and the said regions.

58 * We will at once return the son of Llywelyn, all Welsh hostages, and the charters delivered to us as security for the peace.

59 * With regard to the return of the sisters and hostages of Alexander, king of Scotland, his liberties and his rights, we will treat him in the same way as our other barons of England, unless it appears from the charters that we hold from his father William, formerly king of Scotland, that he should be treated otherwise. This matter shall be resolved by the judgement of his equals in our court.

60 All these customs and liberties that we have granted shall be observed in our kingdom in so far as concerns our own relations with our subjects. Let all men of our kingdom, whether clergy or laymen, observe them similarly in their relations with their own men.

61 * SINCE WE HAVE GRANTED ALL THESE THINGS for God, for the better ordering of our kingdom, and to allay the discord that has arisen between us and our

barons, and since we desire that they shall be enjoyed in their entirety, with lasting strength, for ever, we give and grant to the barons the following security:

The barons shall elect twenty-five of their number to keep, and cause to be observed with all their might, the peace and liberties granted and confirmed to them by this charter.

If we, our chief justice, our officials, or any of our servants offend in any respect against any man, or transgress any of the articles of the peace or of this security, and the offence is made known to four of the said twenty-five barons, they shall come to us – or in our absence from the kingdom to the chief justice – to declare it and claim immediate redress. If we, or in our absence abroad the chief justice, make no redress within forty days, reckoning from the day on which the offence was declared to us or to him, the four barons shall refer the matter to the rest of the twenty-five barons, who may distrain upon and assail us in every way possible, with the support of the whole community of the land, by seizing our castles, lands, possessions, or anything else saving only our own person and those of the queen and our children, until they have secured such redress as they have determined upon. Having secured the redress, they may then resume their normal obedience to us.

Any man who so desires may take an oath to obey the commands of the twenty-five barons for the achievement of these ends, and to join with them in assailing us to the utmost of his power. We give public and free permission to take this oath to any man who so desires, and at no time will we prohibit any man from taking it. Indeed, we will compel any of our subjects who are unwilling to take it to swear it at our command.

If one of the twenty-five barons dies or leaves the country, or is prevented in any other way from discharging his duties, the rest of them shall choose another baron in his place, at their discretion, who shall be duly sworn in as they were.

In the event of disagreement among the twenty-five barons on any matter referred to them for decision, the verdict of the majority present shall have the same validity as a unanimous verdict of the whole twenty-five, whether these were all present or some of those summoned were unwilling or unable to appear.

The twenty-five barons shall swear to obey all the above articles faithfully, and shall cause them to be obeyed by others to the best of their power.

We will not seek to procure from anyone, either by our own efforts or those of a third party, anything by which any part of these concessions or liberties might be revoked or diminished. Should such a thing be procured, it shall be null and void and we will at no time make use of it, either ourselves or through a third party.

62 * We have remitted and pardoned fully to all men any ill-will, hurt or grudges that have arisen between us and our subjects, whether clergy or laymen, since the beginning of the dispute. We have in addition remitted fully, and for our own part have also pardoned, to all clergy and laymen any offences committed as a result of the said dispute between Easter in the sixteenth year of our reign (i.e. 1215) and the restoration of peace.

In addition we have caused letters patent to be made for the barons, bearing witness to this security and to the concessions set out above, over the seals of Stephen archbishop of Canterbury, Henry archbishop of Dublin, the other bishops named above, and Master Pandulf.

63 * IT IS ACCORDINGLY OUR WISH AND COMMAND that the English Church shall be free, and that men in our kingdom shall have and keep all these liberties, rights, and concesssions, well and peaceably in their fulness and entirety for them and their heirs, of us and our heirs, in all things and all places for ever.

Both we and the barons have sworn that all this shall be observed in good faith and without deceit. Witness the abovementioned people and many others.

Given by our hand in the meadow that is called Runnymede, between Windsor and Staines, on the fifteenth day of June in the seventeenth year of our reign (*i.e. 1215: the new regnal year began on 28 May*).